Strategies

FOR READING IN
THE CONTENT AREAS

For information:

Corwin Press
A Sage Publications Company
2455 Teller Road
Thousand Oaks, California 91320
www.corwinpress.com

Sage Publications Ltd.
1 Oliver's Yard
55 City Road
London EC1Y 1SP
United Kingdom

Sage Publications India Pvt. Ltd.
B-42, Panchsheel Enclave
New Delhi 110 017   India

Printed in the United States of America

ISBN 1-57517-859-1

This book is printed on acid-free paper.

05   06   07   08   09   10   9   8   7   6   5   4   3   2   1

Strategies

FOR READING IN THE CONTENT AREAS

Adapted from
Reading and Writing Across Content Areas

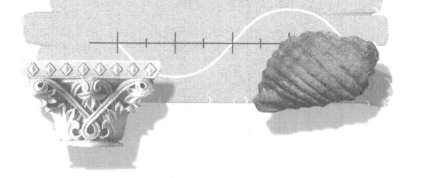

Roberta Sejnost
&
Sharon Thiese

CORWIN PRESS
A SAGE Publications Company
Thousand Oaks, California

$\mathcal{C}$ontents

What Makes a Strategic Reader?

First, strategic readers analyze the task before them by understanding the reading demands made of them and setting a purpose for their reading. In other words, they are able to identify the type of text (narrative or expository) as well as the reading goal to be accomplished. They can read the first chapter or the entire selection. They can readily identify their purpose as reading for pleasure or reading to answer test questions. Next, they are able to initiate a plan of action to achieve that purpose by choosing the strategies they will use as they read. For example, they might choose to skim the material first, identifying the text patterns used; then reread it, making predictions as they go; and finally end by summarizing what they have read. As strategic readers move through this process, they monitor and regulate their comprehension. They recognize that comprehension is occurring because they understand what they are reading. By the same token, if they suddenly become aware that they no longer understand, they know what to do to repair or fix their comprehension problem by rereading a passage, looking up an unfamiliar vocabulary word, or asking a teacher for help. Similarly, if comprehension is progressing well, they may skip sections that contain irrelevant or extraneous details or skim over a passage that contains familiar material.

The Reading Process

As classroom teachers, we are all anxious to help our students develop as strategic readers. Thus, we need to consider what we can do to best foster the strategic reader characteristics described on the previous page.

The good news is that today we know the traditional format is outmoded. No longer is class discussion the primary gauge of reading comprehension. Current educational research supports a format that identifies three stages of reading first observed by Robinson in 1978: *before the text is read, while the text is being read,* and *after the eyes have left the page.* Prereading activities are offered as the first level of support. These activities involve fostering students' prior knowledge. *Prereading* makes students aware of the text structure, helps them identify a purpose for reading, clarifies the vocabulary demands that the text will make, and preteaches a concept that may be difficult. Most importantly, it piques student interest in the reading material.

In the second stage, *during reading,* students interact with their text. In order to make this interaction effective, teachers encourage students to make predictions, keep their purpose for reading in mind, and self-monitor their understanding. Teachers should encourage students to make connections between what they are reading (new knowledge) and what they already know (old knowledge). Instructional frameworks (study guides, graphic organizers) created or provided by the teacher help students accomplish these tasks efficiently. These instructional frameworks are a viable strategy to use in this stage of the reading process.

Finally, in the last stage of the process, *after reading,* students clarify, reinforce, and extend what they have learned. During this stage, students need to organize, synthesize, analyze, and evaluate what they have read so they can easily understand and retrieve important information. In effect, this stage of the reading process allows students to show what they have learned through discussions, presentations, writing activities, research activities, and performances.

Prereading Strategies

As noted earlier, students use prereading strategies before they actually begin reading. The main purpose of these activities is to provide teachers with an opportunity to learn what their students already know about a subject and then help foster adequate prior knowledge so students are mentally ready for instruction. Invaluable as a motivational tool, these activities encourage students to read their assignments.

Word Association

Word Association (Zalaluk, Samuels, and Taylor 1986) is a simple strategy to measure students' prior knowledge about a topic. It is similar to the concept of brainstorming but follows a more definitive procedure. This strategy was developed on the theory that if students have a great deal of prior knowledge about a concept, they should be able to make a number of associations about it. Using this strategy, the teacher supplies students with a keyword and then asks them to make as many associations as they can based on their knowledge of and familiarity with that keyword. Associations can be things, places, events, ideas, etc. However, teachers should discourage students from making associations that are subordinate ideas of the keyword. Focusing on subordinate ideas suggests students are making associations with the words they are generating as associations rather than with the keywords themselves. After students generate the list, the teacher evaluates students' prior knowledge according to the following scale:

0–2 points = low prior knowledge

3–6 points = average prior knowledge

7+ points = high prior knowledge

 ### *Steps for Generating Word Associations*

1. Select a keyword from a topic and tell students to write it on the margin of a piece of paper.

2. Give students three minutes to write down as many words as they can that are related to the keyword. Tell them that they may write down things, places, events, ideas, etc.

3. Award student responses one point for every reasonable association.

4. Tally one additional point for a subordinate idea, but allow students only one additional point no matter how many subordinate ideas they list. Follow this suggestion to discourage students from using generated words rather than keywords.

See Figure 1 for an example of the Word Association strategy.

Example of Word Association

Keyword	Generated Words	
Shark	Ocean	Fins
	Killer	Nurse Shark
	Great White	Tiger Shark
	Live babies	

Total points: 5 points
   1 point for each generated word: ocean, killer, live babies, fins
   1 point for all subordinate words: Great White, Nurse Shark,
     Tiger Shark

Figure 1

Brain Writing

Brain Writing (Rodrigues 1983) is a variation of good old-fashioned brainstorming; however, it follows a more organized procedure and is thus effective in fostering prior knowledge as well as assessing what students already know about a topic.

 Steps for Brain Writing

1. Have students choose a topic (word or concept) about which they will study (research).

2. Instruct students to brainstorm, either individually, in small groups, or as a class, what they know or think they know about the topic and write the information in colored ink on a large sheet of newsprint. (Group breakdown depends on the purpose and structure of the assignment.)

3. Encourage students to share the written information (individuals meet with small group; small group

meets with another small group, etc.). After discussion of the information, have students record any additions, corrections, or comments in a different color ink and award points for information added or corrected.

4. (Optional) Invite the whole class to share knowledge and discuss what is known and what needs to be learned.

5. Instruct students to read (research) to verify or refute knowledge. Allow students to work individually or in collaborative groups.

Knowledge Rating

Knowledge Rating (Blachowicz 1991), while often used as a vocabulary strategy, is also an excellent way to foster prior knowledge about a topic to be studied. There are many variations of this strategy; however, the standard procedure for using Knowledge Rating requires the teacher to provide students with a grid that lists the vocabulary words pertinent to the topic being studied. The teacher then instructs students to show their knowledge of the words by marking: "can define," "have heard," "have seen," "can spell," "can say," and so forth, on the grid. Teachers then ask students to analyze each word. However, teachers can also use this procedure effectively to foster students' prior knowledge by taking it a step further following this procedure.

Steps for Using a Knowledge Rating

See Teacher Tips at the end of this book for an example of a graphic organizer to use with this strategy (Figure 10).

1. Distribute a list of words appropriate to the topic to be studied.

2. Ask students to respond individually to each category by placing an X in the appropriate boxes. Students should be ready to explain or illustrate their responses. Possible categories in addition to those noted above might include "can give an example or an illustration," "can explain," or "can tell how I knew or learned the term."

3. After asking students to respond individually, encourage them to share their responses, first in small groups and then in a whole class discussion.

4. By encouraging students to freely share their responses during the whole class follow-up discussion, the teacher is able to ascertain which terms students know well and foster students' prior knowledge of those terms with which they are unfamiliar.

See Figure 2 for an example of how to help your students evaluate their knowledge of science vocabulary.

Knowledge Rating for Science						
	Have Seen or Heard	Can Say	Can Define	Can Spell	Can Use in a Sentence	Don't Know at All
diffusion	X					
permeable						X
glucose	X	X		X		
dialysis	X	X	X	X	X	
endocytosis						X
phagocytosis						X
impermeable						X
osmosis	X	X	X	X	X	

Figure 2

Anticipation/Prediction Guides

Anticipation Guides (Readance, Bean, and Baldwin 1998) or Prediction Guides (Nichols 1983) help students prepare for the reading they will do. These guides ask them to anticipate or make predictions about the content they will read by responding to a series of statements about that content. However, as in the Knowledge Rating strategy discussed earlier, there are many variations of Anticipation/Prediction Guides. Some guides ask students to respond individually, while others ask students to respond as a small group. Furthermore, some Anticipation Guides ask students to respond to illustrations or graphics as well as written statements.

Anticipation/Prediction Guides are valuable for several reasons. First, the strategy provides a springboard for students to consider the topic to be read, thus fostering prior knowledge. Second, it helps focus interest in the topic, motivating students to read the assigned text. Students are much more interested in reading a selection to see if their predictions are correct than in reading it because the teacher told them to! In addition, making predictions and then reading to confirm or reject them helps students set a purpose for reading. Finally, Readance, Bean, and Baldwin (1998) make the following points: since students make their responses prior to reading, they operate from their experiences and belief systems alone, thus allowing them to respond with little fear of failure due to lack of knowledge. In addition, due to their experiences and belief systems, they might hold preconceived misconceptions about some topics that negatively affect learning. Progressing through the prereading, reading, and postreading stages of this strategy helps alert teachers to these misconceptions and allows them to modify students' knowledge accordingly.

Steps for Using Anticipation/ Prediction Guides

1. Identify those major concepts or details in the selection that students should know or that may challenge or support students' beliefs. Choose statements that stimulate student thinking and interest by presenting concepts about which they may have many opinions but few facts.

2. Leave space next to statements for students to respond (individually, in small groups, or in the whole group).

3. As each statement is discussed, ask students to justify or defend their opinions. Discourage yes/no responses. As an alternative, ask the class to come to a consensus.

4. Instruct students to read the selection.

5. Tell students to revisit the Anticipation/Prediction Guide to determine if they have changed their minds as a result of reading the selection. Have students locate sections in the text that support their new-found knowledge.

6. You may wish to include a column for prediction of author's beliefs.

7. You have the option of using graphics instead of statements.

Figure 3 shows how Anticipation Guides can be used with mathematics.

Anticipation Guide for Mathematics
Anticipation Guide: Percents

Directions

Before reading pages 318 and 319 in your math book, read each statement and place a "yes" by those statements with which you agree and a "no" by those statements with which you disagree under the section labeled *Anticipation.*

Anticipation   **Question**

1._____   Decimals are not whole numbers.

2._____   You can recognize a decimal number because it always has a decimal point.

3._____   Decimal numbers are based on the number 10.

4._____   You line up the decimal point in numbers when you add them.

5._____   You always get a larger number when you multiply decimals.

6._____   Decimals are not related to fractions.

Developed by Nancy Costea, Clarendon Hills Middle School, Clarendon Hills, Illinois.

Figure 3

Directed Reading-Thinking Activity

The Directed Reading-Thinking Activity, also known as the DRTA (Stauffer 1969), is a valuable activity that begins at the prereading stage and continues into the during reading stage until the topic "hooks" students so they proceed on their own. This strategy helps students realize that text is divided into segments, the completion of which can help them better understand the next segments. Students move through a selection by making predictions, reading to validate or reject the predictions made, making new predictions, and repeating the process. The predicting steps help students set a purpose for their reading while the validation/rejection process fosters purposeful reading. Finally, the entire procedure gives students an opportunity to practice their listening and speaking skills since they must reflect aloud and then justify their predictions (Richardson and Morgan 1997). Furthermore, once students become involved in the prediction process, they become motivated to read since, as in the Anticipation Guide strategy discussed previously, they are now reading to verify their own predictions, not because the teacher told them to read!

 ### *Steps for Directed Reading-Thinking Activity (DRTA)*

While the DRTA is often used with narrative texts, it is equally effective with expository texts, which we focus on in this book.

1. Encourage students to activate their prior knowledge by previewing the chapter title, subtitles, charts, maps, pictures, and so on, and sharing what they already know about the topic with the class.

2. Next, ask students to predict what information they think the author will cover in the chapter. Record these predictions on the board. For each prediction, ask the students to support their predictions by posing the question: Why do you think that? or Why is that a possibility? or What makes you think that?

3. Next, direct students to read a section of the chapter silently. After reading, ask students to support their answers by responding to the questions: Which predictions can you prove? Why or why not? This allows them to confirm or reject their predictions.

4. Repeat this cycle until you feel the students can proceed on their own to complete the reading selection.

5. After the selection has been completed, extend learning by asking students to discuss their predictions, noting which ones needed revision and how they were revised. Be sure to ask students how their thinking was influenced by certain sentences or passages.

Sketch to Stretch

Sketch to Stretch (Harste, Short, and Burke 1988) is similar to the DRTA in that it also asks students to monitor their comprehension as they process what they are reading in sections. However, the richness in this strategy lies in the fact that it fosters students' listening skills while engaging their verbal/linguistic, visual/spatial, interpersonal, and intrapersonal intelligences. Teachers ask students to listen to a section of text and sketch what they visualize. Then the teacher distributes copies of the text to read and instructs students to revise their drawings to clarify details or to expand on the meaning after they read.

Next, the students discuss what they have drawn with a peer and focus on what is important to remember from the text. We have adapted this strategy by adding another step. To extend learning, we ask students to reflect on which part of the process was most valuable in helping them understand what was heard or read.

 ### *Steps for Sketch to Stretch*

See Teacher Tips at the end of this book for an example of a graphic organizer to use with this strategy (Figure 11).

1. Read the title of the selection aloud. Have students write what they already know about the topic in the Prediction box.

2. Instruct students to divide a sheet of paper into two boxes for each section to be read.

3. Read one section of the selection aloud and ask students to sketch (in the first box) what comes to mind as they listen.

4. After students complete their sketch, distribute copies of the text for students to read.

5. Advise students to revise the drawings by adding details.

6. When their drawings are complete, ask students to pair off and talk about their sketches, explaining what they were thinking about as they drew. Tell pairs to come to a consensus on what is important to remember from the text they listened to and read.

7. Tell students to summarize these important facts in the second box next to the picture.

8. Repeat this sequence until you feel the students can proceed on their own to complete the reading selection with adequate understanding.

9. As a last step, ask students to identify what aspect of the strategy most contributed to their learning.

During Reading Strategies

During reading strategies are used to help students become active readers and to interact with their text as they read. Two major kinds of during reading strategies are Note Taking and Study Guides.

Note Taking

There are myriad ways students can take notes, but the types that are most successful depend on students being able to identify exactly which ideas are important in the text. Too often students are unable to do this and, as a result, simply take too many notes, causing them to go on information overload. Taking too many notes is as futile as asking students to simply reread text chapters before a test. In order to be successful, students must have read their content area texts, gleaned important concepts, and then encoded that information in their own words. Two ways to help students accomplish this task are the Main Idea I and Structured Note Taking.

Main Idea I

Christen (1987) notes that successful learners must be able to recognize key concepts (main ideas) and organize them into meaningful patterns. In other words, they must be able to locate, select, organize, and remember important information so that they will be able to retrieve it from their long-term memories when needed. An effective way to teach students to do this is the Main Idea I (Christen 1987). Students use a graphic organizer to list three levels of information: the topic, the main idea, and the details. Next, students record their information, limiting it to seven to nine main ideas around any one concept being learned. Then they add a one- or two-sentence summary of the main idea and develop a "teacher-like" main idea question that ties the whole concept together. Using this strategy helps students to recognize important information, process it, and then organize it into a meaningful pattern for later retrieval, all important steps in helping students learn in a brain-compatible way. In addition, this strategy not only fosters the verbal/linguistic and visual/spatial intelligences but also the logical/mathematical ones.

 Steps for Main Idea I

See Teacher Tips at the end of this book for an example of a graphic organizer to use with this strategy (Figure 12).

1. Have students preview a chapter to determine the topic and record it in the upper half of the circle of the Main Idea I graphic organizer. This previewing serves as a mental warm-up for students.

2. Next, instruct students to read a section or several sections to determine the main ideas of the passages read. This step helps students set a purpose for their reading while asking them to be actively involved as they read. Advise students that they should select **no more** than seven to nine main ideas since common knowledge about memory tells us that people can only store seven to nine chunks of information in short-term memory; the rest is "shoved out." This calls for careful teacher planning and guidance in helping students select those seven to nine concepts that are most crucial. *Note:* For each main idea selected, tell students to develop a Main Idea I organizer (see Figure 4 for an example). Direct them to record the main idea in the bottom half of the circle.

3. Tell students to reread the passage and record important details that support each main idea, recording their findings in the portion of the graphic organizer labeled *details.* This step is very valuable since students are asked to revisit the text with a specific purpose in mind. Rereading a text helps bring clarity to the concepts first read. At this point, your students have recorded exactly what information they must learn. The next steps in the process help students process and file the information into their long-term memories for later retrieval.

4. Instruct students to write one or two sentences that summarize the information for each main idea and record it directly under the Main Idea I graphic organizer. This step encourages students to actively process what they have just learned, and the act of writing it down in their own words helps cement the information into their long-term memory.

5. Finally, have students create a "teacher-like" main idea question that resembles a question they might see on a test. Strategic readers constantly interact with the text, asking questions as they read. This process helps students clarify and thus better understand what they are reading.

Figure 4 shows how this strategy can be used with social studies.

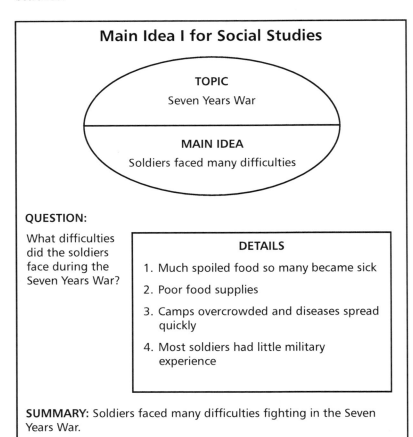

Main Idea I for Social Studies

TOPIC
Seven Years War

MAIN IDEA
Soldiers faced many difficulties

QUESTION:

What difficulties did the soldiers face during the Seven Years War?

DETAILS

1. Much spoiled food so many became sick
2. Poor food supplies
3. Camps overcrowded and diseases spread quickly
4. Most soldiers had little military experience

SUMMARY: Soldiers faced many difficulties fighting in the Seven Years War.

Developed by Sandra Giangrasso, St. Xavier University's Field-Based Master's Program, Hanover Park, Illinois.

Figure 4

SkyLight Professional Development

Structured Note Taking

Structured Note Taking (Smith and Tompkins 1988) is another effective way of helping students determine what information is important to take notes on. In addition, this strategy makes use of graphic organizers to help students visualize the information they are recording, thus clarifying the relationships among ideas for them. The richest aspect of Structured Note Taking, however, is that it helps students learn organizational patterns since the graphic organizer represents the reading selection's major text patterns.

 ### *Steps for Structured Note Taking*

1. To assist your students, preview the selection to determine the organizational pattern used to convey information.

2. Next, create a graphic organizer that follows this pattern, complete with focusing questions, and distribute it as a study guide.

3. Instruct students to read the chapter and take notes by recording the appropriate information in the graphic organizer sections.

Figure 5 shows how this strategy can be used for health.

Structured Note Taking for Health
Categories or Attributes to be Contrasted/Compared

FROSTBITE SYMPTOMS	HEAT STROKE SYMPTOMS
shivering	red, dry skin
white spots	high internal temperature
pain when warming	headaches
numbness	excessive thirst
unconsciousness	dizziness
confusion	nausea

Figure 5

Study/Reading Guides

Another effective during reading strategy is asking students to complete study or reading guides as they read. First, teachers develop Study/Reading Guides to help students focus their attention on the major concepts in a chapter. As a result, students record information that is important rather than extraneous. Secondly, Study/Reading Guides promote active reading since students complete them as they read, rather than after they read. Wood and Mateja (1983) refer to Study/Reading Guides as print tutors.

While there are numerous Study/Reading Guides, two seem to be especially effective for use in content area classrooms: Three Level Guides and Point of View Study Guides.

Three Level Guide

The Three Level Guide (Herber 1978) is an excellent activity to help students become aware of the three levels of comprehension: literal, inferential, and applied. At the literal level, students simply identify the important information in the text or "get the author's message." Although this sounds like an easy task, not all readers are mature or strategic enough to accomplish this feat, and they may need guidance and practice in identifying and answering literal level questions. While it is important to be able to identify important information, strategic readers need to ferret out the author's intended meaning as well. They need to be able to read between the lines, make inferences, and draw conclusions; this is inferential reading. Finally, strategic readers must be able to realize the significance or importance of what is being read and consider how it can be applied to life situations. In other words, they must be able to apply what they have read; they need to be able to read at the applied level of comprehension. Teaching students to use the Three Level Guide fosters all these levels of comprehension.

 Steps for a Three Level Guide

1. Consider what specific ideas, concepts, and interpretations you want students to learn from the text. As you construct this list, focus on statements that reflect the author's intended or inferred meaning. Develop a series of five to six statements from your list; this is level two, the inferential level of your guide. Richardson and Morgan (1997) suggest that teachers may preface statements in this level of the guide with "The author means . . . ."

2. Next, examine the inference statements you developed for level two and determine what explicit facts are needed to support them. Write these as statements for level one of the study guide. Richardson and Morgan (1997) note that often teachers will preface these statements with "The author says . . . ." There should be at least two literal statements to support each major inference.

3. To develop level three, the applied level, construct four to five statements that help students connect prior knowledge to what they have learned. In this section, you want your students to actually apply their new knowledge in some fashion. Richardson and Morgan (1997) explain that these statements can be prefaced with "We can use . . . ."

4. Finally, Vacca and Vacca (1996) suggest that in order to keep students focused as they read, you should add distractors or a misleading fact to levels one and two to discourage students from marking items indiscriminately.

The Three Level Study Guide is a very effective strategy. However, when first using it with students you should model the strategy as a whole class activity. Later, students can do it independently and as a homework assignment. Finally, be careful not to overuse this strategy guide. Not every assignment lends itself to this type of study guide, and any strategy used again and again can become boring.

Figure 6 shows how the Three Level Study Guide can be used with science.

Three Level Study Guide for Science
Baffling Bats

Read pages 127–137 in your textbook. After reading, consider the statements below and place a + in the space next to each statement about bats you think is correct, true, or with which you agree based on what you have read. You will be asked to justify your answers in a class discussion so be sure to locate information from the text to support your answers.

LEVEL I

1. _____ Bats are scary and creepy creatures.
2. _____ Bats and birds are close relatives.
3. _____ Bats can eat 500 insects in an hour.
4. _____ Bats are smart enough to be trained like a dog.
5. _____ There are thirty-nine species of bats in the United States.

LEVEL II

1. _____ Bats cannot fly in the daytime.
2. _____ All bats are dangerous.
3. _____ Bats live in many different places.
4. _____ Bats have arms and fingers and even thumbs!
5. _____ Bats live very short lives.

LEVEL III

1. _____ People should protect bats rather than kill them.
2. _____ Bats help plants grow.
3. _____ Currently some bats in the United States are in danger of becoming extinct.
4. _____ Bats help our environment.
5. _____ We should protect bats so they do not become extinct.

Figure 6

Point of View Study Guide

Another effective study guide is the Point of View Study Guide (Wood 1988), which asks students to assume a role as they read the text. This allows students to gain a different perspective on the reading topic while they enhance their ability to recall and comprehend the information read. In addition, it encourages them to elaborate on the topic by utilizing their prior knowledge. It allows students to put newly acquired information into their own words while learning the content of the selection (Wood, Lapp, and Flood 1992). This strategy follows an interview format by encouraging students to answer the interview questions in their own words, but from the perspective of their assumed roles.

 Steps for Point of View Study Guide

1. Choose a piece of text and brainstorm with the class about a variety of perspectives from which it could be read. For example, in reading a selection on AIDS, students could assume the following perspectives: an AIDS victim, a relative of an AIDS victim, the AIDS virus, a doctor treating an AIDS victim, a boyfriend or girlfriend of an AIDS victim, or a medicine used to treat an AIDS victim.

2. Next, create a series of interview questions that focus on the major content information in the selection.

3. Instruct students to read the text, locating information to answer the interview questions.

4. When students are ready to answer the interview questions, tell them to respond in the first person dialogue format and elaborate as much as they can with information from their personal experience.

This is an exciting activity for students since they are able to become personally involved in the procedure. As an added bonus, students can dress up as characters in the roles they have assumed and act out the interview. Thus, the multiple intelligences of bodily/kinesthetic and visual/spatial are fostered in addition to the verbal/linguistic.

See how the Point of View Study Guide is used for mathematics in Figure 7.

Point of View Study Guide for Mathematics

You are about to be interviewed as if you were a number from the Factor Multiple unit we are studying. Respond to the following questions as if you were a **Factor Tree.**

1. What number are you a factor tree for?
2. I notice that each branch of your tree holds all the factors of this number. Is this always necessary?
3. The bottom row of your tree seems to be all prime numbers. Could you please take a moment of your time to explain what this means?
4. Someone told me that this bottom row has a special name for itself. Do you know anything about this?
   Please explain it to me.

Thanks for your time.
This has been a great interview!

Developed by Diane Wilken, St. Xavier University's Field-Based Master's Program, Hanover Park, Illinois.

Figure 7

After Reading Strategies

While many teachers enrich their students' learning by using *prereading* and *during reading* strategies, far fewer engage students in *after reading* activities. After reading activities serve a definite purpose because they encourage students to think about, reflect on, apply, and sometimes even act upon the knowledge they have learned from their reading. In order to accomplish such action, after reading activities should be varied in nature so students can apply their reading, writing, listening, and speaking skills. The after reading strategies provided help students comprehend and interact with the materials they have read.

Cubing

Cubing, first developed by Cowan and Cowan in 1980, encourages students to look at a topic from various aspects while using their writing and speaking skills to demonstrate knowledge. Vaughan and Estes (1986) propose that students can use the Cubing strategy to improve reading comprehension. For best results, ask students to think of a six-sided cube upon whose sides are written the following: Describe It; Compare It; Associate It; Analyze It; Apply It; and Argue For Or Against It. Then ask them to consider the topic they have studied from these perspectives. These six terms provide a springboard for writing about or discussing an aspect of the topic just studied.

 Steps for Cubing

1. Introduce the topic.

2. Give students five minutes to consider each side of the cube.

3. Ask them to talk or write about the topic from any one of the six possible aspects.

Perspective Cubing

Perspective Cubing (Whitehead 1994) puts a twist on the original cubing strategy by asking students to consider a graphic such as a map, chart, graph, or picture and answer questions related to the following perspectives: space, time, location, culture, talk, and size.

 Steps for Perspective Cubing

Here is a sample activity that can easily be adapted to different subjects and different grade levels.

1. Provide students with a copy of a map. Choose a location or an element of the map such as a river, mountain range, city, village, railroad track, park, or public building. (Your choice should be guided by the content to be studied. For example, if your class is studying the agriculture of Mexico in a geography class, you might focus on the Sierra Madre Mountain Range.)

2. Then, ask students to consider the Sierra Madres from the perspectives of space, time, location, culture, talk, and size. Students can respond to questions you created.

EXAMPLE OF PERSPECTIVE CUBING
Sierra Madre Mountain Range

SPACE

1. What do you think the mountain range looks like as you stand on it? What do you see from where you are?

2. What does it look like from far away? What can you see? Is it large? Small? Hidden in clouds?

TIME

1. What do we know about this mountain range today?

2. What do we think about it today?

3. Pretend this is 500 years in the future. Is the range still here? What does it look like now? How has it changed? What is its importance?

LOCATION

1. What does the mountain range look like from above? From the side? From below?

2. Describe the physical characteristics you can see from each of these different vantage points.

CULTURE

1. What do the citizens of Guadalajara think of this mountain range? What do the citizens of Puerto Vallarta think of this mountain range? What do the citizens of the rest of Mexico think of this mountain range?

2. What do the citizens of the United States think of this mountain range?

3. What do vacationers or travel agents think of this mountain range?

4. What do the citizens of Europe think of this mountain range?

5. What might the first inhabitants (Indians) have thought of this mountain range?

TALK

1. If this mountain range could talk, what story would it tell?

2. Who would it tell its story to?

SIZE

1. If this mountain range could change size, would it get larger, smaller, taller, or shorter?

2. How would its change in size affect our thoughts about it?

Both Cubing and Perspective Cubing appeal to students' creativity, allowing them to demonstrate their knowledge from a variety of perspectives. Since the responses can be either oral or written and done individually or in a small group, students utilize verbal/linguistic, visual/spatial, intrapersonal, and interpersonal intelligences. See Figure 8 for topic ideas across content areas.

Suggestions for Cubing and Perspective Cubing Topics			
Social Studies	Mathematics	Science	Health/PE
Manifest Destiny	prime numbers	diffusion	AIDS
democracy	equation	osmosis	respiration
fascism	polynomial	nucleus	digestion
isolationism	factor	evolution	immunity
communism	simplify	photosynthesis	contagion

Figure 8

Magnet Summaries

Summaries, as we know, are merely brief statements that contain the essential ideas from longer passages or selections. While this sounds like a simple task, as teachers we know that writing a summary is often not a simple task at all. In fact, in working with academically challenged students, we have discovered that the greatest challenge they have is deciding which details are important and which can be eliminated. An excellent after reading strategy that encourages summarizing while improving students' writing skills is Magnet Summaries (Buehl 1995). In order to complete the Magnet Summaries strategy, students must first identify keywords from the passages read. Once these keywords have been determined, the students use them to develop a summary of the passage.

 ### Steps for a Magnet Summary

See Teacher Tips at the end of this book for an example of a graphic organizer to use with this strategy (Figure 13).

1. After assigning a passage to be read, help students determine some keywords from the passage. Keywords relate directly to the concept being taught.

2. Explain to students that these keywords are like magnets in that they attract information that is important to the topic.

3. Next, ask students to recall details from the passage that are connected to the magnet words. Both the word and the details should be recorded on a 3 x 5 index card.

4. After students have recorded their magnet words and supporting details on cards, show them how the information can be developed into a short summary. Strive to have students develop a one-sentence summary whenever possible.

5. Once all the cards have been summarized, ask students to arrange their sentences in logical order to develop a coherent summary. Remind students that they may have to edit sentences so their summaries will flow smoothly.

SkyLight Professional Development

The Magnet Summaries strategy provides many advantages as an after reading strategy. While it gives students practice in expressing key concepts in their own words, its greatest value lies in providing a logical and simple procedure for helping students determine relevant and irrelevant details as they synthesize the information. While this strategy appears simple, its success depends on teacher modeling to guide students through the process before they produce Magnet Summaries independently. See Figure 9 for an example of Magnet Summaries.

Magnet Summary for Social Studies

migrate   exploration   magnetic compass
Keywords

CULTURAL CONTACTS
Magnet Word

Ice Age   political situations   travel   trade
Keywords

Summary Statement:
Cultural contacts came as a result of travel and trade. Inventions, like the magnetic compass, made travel to and trade with new places easier which, in turn, led to migration when bad weather, like the Ice Age, or harsh political situations threatened.

Figure 9

Socratic Questioning

A very effective after reading strategy that asks students to use their listening and speaking skills is Socratic Questioning. As classroom teachers we are, perhaps, familiar with Sir Francis Bacon's wise words, "Reading maketh a full man; conference a ready man; and writing an exact man." Yet how often do we successfully engage students in conference? For most students, classroom discussions are a time to answer the teacher's questions with a brief response. Often these discussions are not a time to delve into, reflect upon, and extend the concepts presented in the question in a lively, animated, high-level conversation. This, however, is exactly what we need to encourage our students to do; they need to learn to ask why, to explore their own personal beliefs about a concept, and to listen, analyze, and reflect upon what others say about that concept and respond. The Socratic Questioning strategy, which is based on Socrates' belief that students must learn to think for themselves rather than just get the right answer, encourages critical thinking.

 ### *Steps for Socratic Questioning*

1. Students read a text rich in ideas, issues, and values, which will stimulate thought and dialogue.

2. After reading, the dialogue is opened with a question, which may be posed by the leader or any of the participants. This question has no "official" correct answer but, instead, leads the students into thoughtful reflection and new questions.

3. The success of the discussion depends on the students' abilities to read analytically, listen carefully, reflect on the questions asked, and ask critical, thought-provoking questions in response.

EXAMPLE OF SOCRATIC QUESTIONING

Fogarty (1997) provides an extensive list of questions that are effective in Socratic Questioning.

- What reasons do you have for saying that?
- Why do you agree or disagree with that point?
- How are you defining the term?
- What do you mean by that expression?
- Is what you're saying now consistent with what you said before?
- Could you clarify that comment?
- When you said that, what was implied by your remarks?
- What follows from what you just said?
- Is it possible that you are contradicting each other?
- Could you clarify that remark?
- Are you sure that you are not contradicting yourself?
- What alternatives are there?
- Could you give an example of that?
- Are you familiar with incidents of this sort?
- Why did you find that interesting?
- Are you saying . . . ?
- I wonder if what you're saying is . . . ?
- So, you see it as . . . ?
- Is that the point you're making?
- Can I sum up what you've said by . . . ?
- Are you suggesting . . . ?
- If you're correct, would it follow . . . ?

- The implications of what you've said seem far reaching if . . . then . . . ?
- Aren't you assuming . . . ?
- Is what you've just said based on . . . ?
- What is your reason for saying that . . . ?
- Why do you believe . . . ?
- What can you say in defense of that view?
- How do you know?
- Couldn't it also be . . . ?
- What if someone . . . ?

From *Brain-Compatible Classrooms* by Robin Fogarty. © 1997 SkyLight Training and Publishing, Inc. Reprinted by permission of SkyLight Professional Development.

Teacher Tips

1. As a review, place students in groups of three and assign them a section of a chapter to read. After reading, have students practice the Structured Note Taking strategy by identifying the pattern of organization used to construct the passage and then developing a graphic organizer to match that pattern. Finally, have students create the graphic organizer and flesh it out with details. The completed organizer can then be printed as an overhead transparency, with each group presenting their organizer to the class to highlight the important points of the chapter.

2. Have students brainstorm different points of view that can be taken when reading a textbook selection. Make a collection of these differing viewpoints to use when assigning the Point of View Study Guide strategy for students to complete.

3. Place students in groups and assign them a section of a chapter to read. When they have completed the section, ask them to create a Magnet Summary to summarize the important points of the chapter. These Magnet Summaries can be keyboarded, printed, and compiled for use as a review of the chapter.

4. Use the graphic organizers provided for the following strategies:

   a. Knowledge Rating (Figure 10)

   b. Organizer for Sketch to Stretch (Figure 11)

   c. Main Idea I (Figure 12)

   d. Magnet Summary (Figure 13)

Knowledge Rating

Directions: In the space provided, write the words your teacher has chosen. Respond individually to each category by placing an X in the appropriate boxes. Be ready to explain or illustrate your responses

Word	Have Seen or Heard	Can Say	Can Define	Can Spell	Can Use in a Sentence	Don't Know at All

Figure 10   Based on Blachowicz 1991

Organizer for Sketch to Stretch

Directions: Listen as your teacher reads the title of the selection. Think of what you already know about the topic you will be reading about. Write about it in the section entitled Prediction. Next, listen as your teacher reads a section of text aloud. Sketch what comes to mind as you listen. After you complete your sketch, you will receive a copy of text to read. You can revise the drawings by adding details. Then, you can pair off with a classmate and talk about your sketches, explaining what you were thinking about as you drew. Arrive at a consensus about what is important to remember from the text you listened to and read. Summarize these important facts in the box next to the picture.

Prediction:

Sketch	Summary of Important Points
Sketch	Summary of Important Points
Sketch	Summary of Important Points

Figure 11

Main Idea I

Directions: Preview a chapter of text to determine the topic and record it in the space provided. Then, read a section to determine the main idea. Reread the passage, and record important details that support each main idea. Record your findings in the portion of the graphic organizer labeled details. Write one or two sentences that summarize the information for each main idea and record it in the appropriate section. Finally, create a "teacher-like" main idea question that you might see on a test about the material you are studying. Write questions at several levels: literal, inferential, evaluative, and applied.

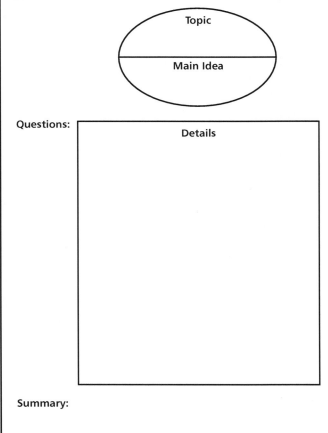

Topic

Main Idea

Questions:

Details

Summary:

Figure 12

Magnet Summary

Directions: Select a keyword from the passage. Write the keyword (Magnet Word) in the middle of the page and record pertinent details at the top and bottom. Finally, write a summary statement in the space provided.

——— ——— ——— ——— ———

Keywords

———————

Magnet Word

——— ——— ——— ——— ———

Keywords

Summary Statement:

Figure 13

Bibliography

Blachowicz, C. L. Z. 1991. Vocabulary instruction in content classes for special needs learners: Why and how? *Journal of Reading, Writing, and Learning Disabilities International* 7(4): 297–308.

Buehl, D. 1995. *Classroom strategies for interactive learning.* Schofield, WI: Wisconsin State Reading Association.

Christen, W. L. 1987. *The A.T.L.A.S.S. program: The application of teaching and learning and study skills.* Phoenix, AZ: Universal, Dimensions, Inc.

Cowan, G., and E. Cowan. 1980. *Writing.* New York: Wiley.

Fogarty, R. 1997. *Brain-compatible classrooms.* Arlington Heights, IL: SkyLight Training and Publishing.

Harste, J., K. Short, and C. Burke. 1988. *Creating classrooms for authors.* Portsmouth, NH: Heinemann

Herber, H. 1978. *Teaching reading in the content areas.* 2nd ed. Englewood Cliffs, NJ: Prentice Hall.

Paris, S. G., M. Y. Lipson, and K. K. Wixson. 1983. Becoming a strategic reader. *Contemporary Educational Psychology* 8(3) 293–316.

Readence, J. E., T. W. Bean, and R. S. Baldwin. 1998. *Content area literacy: An integrated approach.* Dubuque, IA: Kendall/Hunt Publishing Co.

Richardson, J. S., and R. F. Morgan. 1997. *Reading to learn in the content areas.* Belmont, CA: Wadsworth Publishing Co.

Robinson, H.A. 1978. *Facilitating successful reading strategies.* Paper presented at International Reading Association, Houston, Texas.

Rodrigues, R. J. 1983. Tools for developing prewriting skills. *English Journal* 72(2): 58–60.

Smith, P., and G. Tompkins. 1988. Structured notetaking: A new strategy for content area readers. *Journal of Reading* 32(1): 46–53.

Stauffer, R. G. 1969. *Directing reading maturity as a cognitive process*. New York: Harper & Row.

Vacca, R. T. and J. L. Vacca. 1996. *Content area reading*. Boston: Allyn and Bacon.

Vaughan, J., and T. Estes. 1986. *Reading and reasoning beyond the primary grades*. Boston: Allyn and Bacon.

Whitehead, D. 1994. Teaching literacy and learning strategies through a modified guided silent reading procedure. *Journal of Reading* 38(1): 24–30.

Wood. K. D. 1988. Guiding students through informational text. *The Reading Teacher* 41(9): 912–20.

Wood, K. D., D. Lapp, and J. Flood. 1992. *Guiding readers through text: A review of study guides*. Newark, DE: International Reading Association.

Wood, K. D., and J. A. Mateja, 1983. Adapting secondary level strategies for use in elementary classrooms. *The Reading Teacher* 36:392–395.

Zalaluk, B. L., S. J. Samuels, and B. M. Taylor. 1986. A simple technique for estimating prior knowledge. *Journal of Reading* 30(1): 56–60.

**CORWIN
PRESS**

The Corwin Press logo—a raven striding across an open book—represents the union of courage and learning. Corwin Press is committed to improving education for all learners by publishing books and other professional development resources for those serving the field of PreK–12 education. By providing practical, hands-on materials, Corwin Press continues to carry out the promise of its motto: **"Helping Educators Do Their Work Better."**